Jennifer Frost

I hope you enjoy this book as much as I have!

"Attitude is a little thing that makes a big difference."
~Winston Churchill

Holly

The POWER OF ATTITUDE

MAC ANDERSON

BY THE FOUNDER OF *Successories*®

simple truths®
THE GIFT OF INSPIRATION

Naperville, IL 60563
www.simpletruths.com

Published by Simple Truths, LLC
1952 McDowell Road, Suite 300
Naperville, IL 60563-65044

Design: Koechel Peterson and Associates, Inc., Mpls, MN

Printed and bound in the United States of America.

ISBN 978-1-60810-005-7

www.simpletruths.com
(800) 900-3427

10   WOZ   12

table of contents

ATTITUDE

IS EVERYTHING

Destiny is not a matter of chance, it is a matter of choice. It is not a thing to be waited for, it is a thing to be achieved.

WILLIAM
JENNINGS BRYAN

IN MANY WAYS, WE'RE ALIKE; however, one little difference almost always makes a big difference. The little difference is attitude.

William James, over a century ago, said, "The greatest discovery of this generation is that a human being can alter their life by altering their attitude." I believe this with all my heart, and over the years have seen it happen countless times. What most people fail to realize is that your attitude not only impacts your happiness and your success, it also can impact the happiness and success of all the people around you . . . your family, your friends, and your peers at work. Attitudes truly are contagious, and from time to time we need to ask ourselves . . . "is mine worth catching?"

There is no way to overstate the importance of a positive attitude in your life. However, no one can underestimate the difficulty in maintaining it. It's not easy, and it's a very personal thing, but it can be done.

The Power of Attitude was written with that in mind. I only can share with you what works for me in developing and maintaining a positive approach to life. My goal is that some of the ideas and stories I'll share will inspire you to live the life of your dreams and to make a positive difference in the lives of others.

It's my hope that this book will be a useful tool in helping you:

- Manage your energy levels
- Keep your soul alive
- Take new paths
- Reduce stress
- Develop the "Human Touch"
- Attack your fears
- Live in awe
- Savor small successes
- Burn brightly without burning out
- Hang on when the storms blow through

Most importantly, I'd ask you to keep this book handy, so whenever you feel a little down, pick it up and read a few pages. I guarantee it will make you feel better for the journey ahead. I wish you the best!

Mac Anderson

PASSION

WHEREVER YOU CHOOSE TO GO,
GO THERE WITH ALL YOUR HEART.

PASSION FUELS
Enthusiasm

Nothing great was ever accomplished without enthusiasm.

RALPH WALDO

EMERSON

A BELLMAN MADE MY DAY RECENTLY. After checking into an Atlanta hotel, Sam (his name was on his badge) picked up my two bags, gave a big smile, and said, "Isn't it a gorgeous day today?" I nodded and said, "Sure is." He then said, "I just spent the entire weekend with my two grandkids, and I can't remember when I've had more fun. Aren't kids great?" I nodded again, and said, "They are special," and then I added, "Sam, it seems like you're having a great day." He then looked up with a grin I'll never forget and said, "Mr. Anderson, every day above ground is a great day!"

I walked into my room feeling recharged by Sam's enthusiasm. It was obvious that he had chosen to live life to the fullest, and given the opportunity to touch someone's life in a positive way, my bet is that he took it, every time.

Every day we all have that same opportunity to make

a positive difference in the lives of others. We can choose to mope about our lot in life, or we can decide to live in awe, touching hearts along the way.

Ah, yes . . . we all know ducks who make lots of noise, quacking and complaining about their problems in life. And then there are eagles, who go about their business and consistently soar above the crowd.

Thanks, Sam, for soaring into my life.

When we choose not to focus on what is missing from our lives
but are grateful for the abundance that's present . . .
we experience heaven on earth.
SARAH BREATHNACH

A JOURNEY OF A THOUSAND MILES
BEGINS WITH A SINGLE STEP.

CHINESE PROVERB

DREAMS

IT IS *Never* TOO LATE

OUR ATTITUDE in many ways ties directly to our "inner voice" that forever asks the question . . . "Are you moving toward your dream?" If your answer is "yes," then hope breeds contentment. However, if the answer is "no, it's too late," despair may fester within your subconscious. You might not even realize why your life lacks joy.

I can say this with conviction . . . "It is never too late to be what you could have been." Dreams are free, and just having them can make your life worth living.

Ray Kroc is one of my business heroes. He founded McDonald's when he was 52 years old, after trying for over two years and talking to more than one hundred people to raise the money. Fifteen years ago, I had the good fortune of talking to Tom Seay, one of the potential investors whom Ray approached. Tom told me how Ray had come to his office one Friday afternoon with his business plan for this "crazy idea" called McDonald's. For $100,000 he was offering Tom thirty percent of the company. Tom told him that he didn't have the time to review it then but that he would take it home over the weekend.

Monday morning rolled around, and Ray was waiting at the front door when Tom got to his office. Tom invited him in and said, "Ray, I read this plan three times; even shared it with a friend. And we both decided that there's no way in the world you can make any money selling hamburgers."

We all know that Ray thought otherwise; and the rest, of course, is history.

*The only things that stand between a person
and what they want in life are the will to try it
and the faith to believe it's possible.*

RICH DeVOS

Imperfect action is better than perfect inaction.

HARRY TRUMAN

DO IT NOW

EXPECT THE BEST

IT'S A FUNNY THING ABOUT LIFE;

IF YOU REFUSE TO ACCEPT

ANYTHING BUT THE BEST,

YOU VERY OFTEN GET IT.

W. SOMERSET MAUGHN

UNDERSTAND THIS
Life-changing Law

A NATIVE AMERICAN BOY was talking with his grandfather. "What do you think about the world situation?" he asked. The grandfather replied, "I feel like wolves are fighting in my heart. One is full of anger and hatred; the other is full of love, forgiveness, and peace." "Which one will win?" asked the boy. To which the grandfather replied, "The one I feed." (Origin Unknown)

This simple story provides the essence of a life–changing law of the universe . . . *You become what you think about.* The words are almost too simple to "feel important." However, if you "get it," if you truly understand their meaning, you can forever harness the power of a positive attitude.

Simply stated . . . if we choose to think positive thoughts, we'll get positive results; if we think negative thoughts, we'll get negative results. Pretend for a moment that every thought is a seed you sow in your fertile mind. Therefore, as I once heard someone say, "If you plant crabapples, don't expect to harvest Golden Delicious." You will reap the fruit of the thoughts you sow.

In his best–selling classic *The Power of Positive Thinking,* Dr. Norman Vincent Peale wrote:

"Learn to expect, not to doubt. In doing so you bring everything into the realm of possibility . . . It is amazing how a sustained expectation of the best sets the forces in motion which cause the best to materialize."

Whether you think you can,
or think you can't . . . you're right.

HENRY FORD

First we make our attitudes. Then our attitudes make us.

DENNIS WAITLEY

ATTITUDE

SUCCESS

IT'S NOT THE
THINGS YOU GET
BUT THE HEARTS
YOU TOUCH
THAT WILL
DETERMINE YOUR
SUCCESS IN LIFE.

THE *Dash*

The heart that gives, gathers.

HANNA MOORE

A FEW WEEKS AGO I received a note from Anna Lee Wilson. She is a Successories franchisee and is one of the kindest, most caring people I've ever met. In the note she said, "I've enclosed a copy of my favorite poem. I think you'll like it." She was right. It's **"The Dash,"** by Linda Ellis.*

I read of a man who stood to speak
At the funeral of a friend
He referred to the dates on her tombstone
From the beginning to the end

He noted that first came her date of birth
And spoke the following date with tears,
But he said what mattered most of all
Was the dash between those years. (1934–1998)

For that dash represents all the time
That she spent alive on earth.
And now only those who loved her
Know what that little line is worth.

For it matters not, how much we own;
The cars, the house, the cash,
What matters is how we live and love
And how we spend our dash.

So think about this long and hard.
Are there things you'd like to change?
For you never know how much time is left,
That can still be rearranged.

If we could just slow down enough
To consider what's true and real,
And always try to understand
The way other people feel.

And be less quick to anger,
And show appreciation more
And love the people in our lives
Like we've never loved before.

If we treat each other with respect,
And more often wear a smile
Remembering that this special dash
Might only last a little while.

So, when your eulogy's being read
With your life's actions to rehash
Would you be proud of the things they say
About how you spent your dash?

* This poem touched
my heart so much that
I called Linda Ellis to
thank her for writing
it. Our conversation
took us down a
wonderful path . . .
to partner in creating
a gift book based on
"The Dash." One of
the great things I love
about life is that when
you wake up each
morning you never
know who you might
meet who will make a
positive difference.

SMILE

A SMILE IS THE LIGHT ON YOUR FACE THAT LETS SOMEONE KNOW YOU'RE HOME.

THE *Good News* GIRL

ONE OF THE MOST WONDERFUL things about having a positive attitude is the number of people it touches, many times in ways you'll never know.

Recently, I stopped by a convenience store to get a newspaper and a pack of gum. The young woman at the check–out counter said, "That'll be five dollars please," and as I reached into my wallet, the thought occurred to me that a newspaper and gum didn't quite make it to five dollars. When I looked up to get a "re–quote," she had a big smile on her face and said, "Gotcha! I got to get my tip in there somehow!" I laughed when I knew I'd been had. She then glanced down at the paper I was buying and said, "I'm sick and tired of all this negative stuff on the front pages. I want to read some good news for a change." She then said, "In fact, I think someone should just publish a *Good News* newspaper—a paper with wonderful, inspirational stories about people overcoming adversity and doing good things for others. I'd buy one every day!" She then thanked me for coming in and said, "Maybe we'll get lucky tomorrow; maybe we'll get some good news," and she laughed. She made my day.

The following day after my business appointments, I dropped by the same store again to pick up bottled water, but a different young lady was behind the counter. As I checked out I said, "Good afternoon" and handed her my money for the water. She said nothing—not a word, not a smile . . . nothing. She just handed me my change and in a negative tone ordered . . . "Next!"

It hit me right between the eyes: Two people, same age; one made me feel great, and the other, well, made me feel that I had inconvenienced her by showing up.

By the choices we make, by the attitudes we exhibit, we are influencing lives every day in positive or negative ways . . . our family, our peers, our friends, and even strangers we've never met before and will never meet again.

So when you brush your teeth every morning, look in the mirror and ask yourself this important question, *Who do I want to be today? "The Grouch"* or *"The Good News Girl?"* Your answer will go a long way toward determining the joy and happiness that you will experience in your life.

Attitude is a little thing that makes a big difference.

ATTITUDE

COURAGE DOES NOT ALWAYS ROAR.

SOMETIMES IT IS THE QUIET VOICE

AT THE END OF THE DAY,

SAYING, "I WILL TRY AGAIN TOMORROW."

COURAGE

PULL THE *Weeds*

Courage is a door that can only be opened from the inside.

TERRY NEIL

WHEN I WAS IN HIGH SCHOOL, I loved playing football. It was, and still is, my favorite sport. But there was one part I hated . . . those first two weeks of practice in August, when the temperature often hit 100 degrees. Coach Kilzer, however, knew the importance of those two weeks and he "took no prisoners" . . . the agility drills, the grueling windsprints, and finally the dreaded laps. I still have nightmares about those five laps around the field in full pads following a three–hour workout. My body after those first few days was so sore I could hardly get out of bed each morning. But as each day passed, the pain would lessen, and after three or four weeks, the transformation of being in "football shape" would happen.

Breaking bad habits is no different. The physical and mental pain can be grueling, whether you're trying to exercise more, smoke less, drink less, eat healthier, or work less . . . it's never easy. But the benefits to your health and to your attitude can be priceless. Breaking a habit starts with courage, ends with discipline, and is fueled by desire.

I saw this recently, and would like to share it with you.

I am your constant companion.
I am your greatest asset or heaviest burden.
I will push you up to success or down to disappointment.
I am at your command.
Half the things you do might just as well be turned over to me,
For I can do them quickly, correctly, and profitably.
I am easily managed, just be firm with me.
Those who are great, I have made great.
Those who are failures, I have made failures.
I am not a machine, though I work with the precision of a
Machine and the intelligence of a person.
You can run me for profit, or you can run me for ruin.
Show me how you want it done. Educate me. Train me.
Lead me. Reward me.
And I will then . . . do it automatically.
I am your servant.
Who am I?
I am a habit.

The author of the above is unknown, but the words are right on target. If you make good habits, they in turn will make you. But like the weeds in the garden, bad habits can take over your life. Make a decision today to pull those weeds.

GOALS

TAKE THE LONG VIEW . . .

ONE DAY AT A TIME.

THE POWER
Of Goals

FIND A PURPOSE and your passion will follow. But write it down, and read it often.

I got this lesson early in my life. I was a freshman at Murray State University in Murray, Kentucky, and was recruited by my friend Eddie Grogan to sell books for the Southwestern Company. They had been in business for over 100 years and each summer hired several thousand college students. Eddie had done well the summer before and made four times as much as I had working at a men's clothing store. I was excited and wanted to try it for the new experience and for the additional money. There was one small problem, though. My Dad didn't want me to do it. Not only did he not want me to do it . . . he didn't think I *could* do it!

Well, that was it. I now had a mission. The son was going to prove the father wrong.

As summer approached, however, I began to have doubts. Furthermore, I realized it was going to be hard work—over sixty hours a week for three months. Maybe I didn't have the discipline or maybe I couldn't handle the rejection of selling door–to–door.

In the end, however, I decided to give it a shot. The opportunity to prove my Dad wrong overpowered my doubts and fears. I then made an impulsive decision that would hold the key to my success that summer. I wrote myself a letter and promised myself I'd read it every day. I still have it, and here's what it said:

Dear Mac,

This is the chance of a lifetime. You'll find out what you're made of. Your Dad doesn't think you can do it. You can prove him wrong. It won't be easy and I'm sure there will be many times you'll want to quit. Hang in there with every fiber of persistence that you can muster.

At the end of the summer when you look in the mirror . . . say with pride . . . I did it.

Make him proud to say, this is my son.

Well, did I make him proud? You bet I did. Out of several thousand college students from schools all over the country, I ranked seventh in sales for the summer. But more importantly, I made myself proud. I proved that I had the guts and the discipline to stick it out. It was also a giant boost to my self—esteem.

The question I've asked myself many times is . . . would I have succeeded without the letter? And the answer in my mind always comes back . . . No! Without question, this was the most difficult job I've ever had in my life. The hours were long, the rejection was tough, and there were at least a dozen times in the first month that I wanted to quit.

I am 100 percent convinced that the difference in my success or failure that summer was those 84 words I wrote on a sheet of notebook paper. The lessons I learned were powerful: discipline, hard work, goals. But most of all I learned the power of words . . . when tied to a purpose.

A goal, not in writing, is simply a wish.

LAUGHTER

THE EARTH LAUGHS IN FLOWERS.

RALPH WALDO EMERSON

Laugh Loud
AND OFTEN

*Laughter is sunshine
in any life.*

WILLIAM THACKERY

LAUGHTER IS TO THE SOUL what soap is to the body. In fact, researchers suggest that we need a minimum of twelve laughs a day just to stay healthy. It can affect our brain chemistry and immune system in very positive ways. It also can be powerful in providing positive energy that can fight off negative thoughts.

Here's an exercise I want you to try the next time you're in the car alone and feel a little down in the dumps. When you hit an open stretch of road—or you might prefer to pull over and park—start laughing as loud and hard as you can for one solid minute. Not thirty seconds, but a full minute. Once you start it becomes easy to keep going because your brain is thinking . . . *this is one of the nuttiest things I've ever done.* When you finally stop you will feel like a new person. The frown will have been transformed into a smile and the endorphins in your brain will have kicked in. It works. I guarantee it, because I've done it many times. Now, here's a little tip . . . don't do it at stop lights, because a big, sensitive guy in the car next to you might think you're laughing at him. If that were to happen it could affect your "health" in a negative way.

Southwest Airlines does a wonderful job of laughing with their team, with their customers, and at themselves. About six months ago I was on a flight when the flight attendant announced over the P.A. system: "Today we have a gentleman on board who's celebrating his 99th birthday, and this is the first time he's ever flown." As you can imagine, the cabin broke out in light applause. Then she said, "Now on the way out, stop by the cockpit and wish him 'happy birthday'." Beautiful! It made my day. Everyone on board roared with laughter.

Laugh loud, and laugh often. It'll keep you happy, keep you healthy, and keep your attitude headed in a positive direction.

FAITH

BEAUTIFUL LIGHT IS BORN OF DARKNESS,
SO THE FAITH THAT SPRINGS FROM CONFLICT
IS OFTEN THE STRONGEST AND BEST.
R. TURNBULL

KEEP THE *Faith*

EVEN WITH GOALS, passion, and purpose in our lives, we're all faced with adversity . . . and how we react to adversity will dictate our success or failure. There are many roadblocks, detours, and potholes along the way. Sometimes your courage may wane, and your heart may doubt. You'll want to quit. You'll need all the help you can find to get through these difficult times.

I know because as an entrepreneur, living my dream, I've been there. Some of the greatest inspirations that I draw on during tough times are examples from those who have gone before me. People who have faced setbacks, and yet had the courage and the strength to persevere . . . to hang on while the storms blew through.

Persistence kept Walt Disney pursuing his dreams, despite having to declare bankruptcy five times.

Although Helen Keller had every reason in the world to feel sorry for herself, she chose not to. Her persistence despite overwhelming odds still gives inspiration to millions of people.

The example of Abe Lincoln, however, provides some of my greatest motivation. His setbacks were devastating. He failed in business in 1831. He was defeated for state legislature in 1832. He tried another business in '33. It failed. His fiancé died in '35. He had a nervous breakdown in '36. In '43 he ran for Congress and was defeated. He tried again in '48 and was defeated again. He tried running for the Senate in '55. He lost. The next year he ran for vice president and lost. In '59 he ran for the Senate again and was defeated again. Finally in 1860,

Abraham Lincoln was elected the sixteenth president of the United States, and you know the rest of the story.

Recently I visited with Mark Victor Hanson, co–author of *Chicken Soup For The Soul*. Mark shared his story of approaching thirty–five different publishers before the thirty–sixth finally said "Yes" and sold seventy–five million copies, making it one of the best selling book series of all time. Just think, thirty–five people said, "No . . . We don't want your book." What if Mark had decided to quit after the nineteenth, twenty–fifth or even the thirty–fourth? Mark's unwavering passion for the project gave him the fuel and the courage to persevere. And as a result hundreds of positive, real life stories have inspired millions of people.

Passion, belief, and self–trust are the fuel for a positive attitude that causes us to be totally committed to a goal. Giving up is not an option.

GOLDEN RULE

IF YOU TEACH YOUR
CHILD THE GOLDEN
RULE, YOU WILL HAVE
LEFT AN ESTATE OF
INCALCULABLE VALUE.

REMEMBER RULE #1 . . .
It's Golden

I GREW UP IN TRENTON, a west Tennessee town of five thousand people. I have wonderful memories of those first eighteen years, and many people in Trenton influenced my life in very positive ways. My football coach, Walter Kilzer, taught me the importance of hard work, discipline, and believing in myself. My history teacher, Fred Culp, is still the funniest person I've ever met. He taught me that a sense of humor, and especially laughing at yourself, can be one of life's greatest blessings.

But my father was my hero. He taught me many things, but at the top of the list, he taught me to treat people with love and respect . . . to live the Golden Rule. I remember one particular instance of him teaching this "life lesson" as if it were yesterday. Dad owned a furniture store, and I used to dust the furniture every Wednesday after school to earn my allowance. One afternoon I observed my Dad talking to all the customers as they came in . . . the hardware store owner, the banker, a farmer, a doctor. At the end of the day, just as Dad was closing, the garbage collector came in.

I was ready to go home, and I thought that surely Dad wouldn't spend too much time with him. But I was wrong. Dad greeted him at the door with a big hug and talked with him about his wife and son who had been in a car accident the month before. He empathized, he asked questions, he listened, and he listened some more. I kept looking at the clock, and when the man finally left, I asked, "Dad, why did you spend so much time with him? He's just the garbage collector." Dad then looked at me, locked the front door to the store, and said, "Son, let's talk."

He said, "I'm your father and I tell you lots of stuff as all fathers should, but if you remember nothing else I ever tell you, remember this . . . treat every human being just the way that you would want to be treated." He said, "I know this is not the first time you've heard it, but I want to make sure it's the first time you truly understand it, because if you had understood, you would never have said what you said." We sat there and talked for another hour about the meaning and the power of the Golden Rule. Dad said, "If you live the Golden Rule everything else in life will usually work itself out, but if you don't, your life probably will be very unhappy and without meaning."

I recently heard someone say, "If you teach your child the Golden Rule, you will have left them an estate of incalculable value." Truer words were never spoken.

Resolve to be tender with the young, compassionate with the aged,

sympathetic with the striving, and tolerant with the weak . . .

because in your life you will have been all of these.

COMPASSION

GIVING

SERVICE IS THE VERY PURPOSE OF LIFE.
IT IS THE RENT WE PAY
FOR BEING ON THIS PLANET.
MARION WRIGHT EDELMAN

SHARE *Yourself*

ONE OF MY FAVORITE HABITS in life is waking up early on Sunday morning, getting the Sunday paper, making a hot cup of coffee, and kicking back to read about what's going on in the world. It's my quiet time . . . my time alone to reflect and relax.

One Sunday morning about halfway through my little ritual, I spotted a headline that read "Graduating Student Credits His 'Angel'" . . . and I began to read.

A young man who was graduating from college told the story about how Oral Lee Brown was his "Real Life Angel." In 1987 Brown, a real estate agent in Northern California, saw a young girl in her neighborhood begging for money.

When she went to the school the girl had claimed to attend, Brown couldn't find her, but that day she made a decision that would change the lives of many other children forever. She adopted an entire first–grade class in one of Oakland's lowest performing schools, and she pledged that she personally would pay for anyone who wanted to attend college.

This would be a great story even if Oral Lee Brown was independently wealthy; however, it is a much greater story considering she was a former cotton picker from Mississippi, making $45,000 a year and raising two children of her own.

Brown lived up to her pledge. Since 1987, she's personally saved $10,000 a year while raising donations for her "adopted first–grade kids." And because of her tremendous act of unselfish love, children who could have been "swallowed by the streets" are now graduating from college to pursue their dreams.

We all seek our purpose in life. Most of us wonder how we can make a positive difference during our brief time on this earth. But *asking* and *doing* are different things.

It's hard to imagine that Oral Lee Brown wouldn't have a wonderful positive attitude, because she has thought less about herself and more about others. This, in my opinion, is a "little secret" that many people never quite understand about life.

It is one of the most beautiful compensations in life . . .
we can never help another without helping ourselves.

RALPH WALDO EMERSON

SERVING

JOY

LIFE MUST BE LIVED AS PLAY.

PLATO

Manage Stress
BEFORE IT
MANAGES YOU

The sovereign invigorator of the body is exercise, and of all the exercises walking is the best.

THOMAS

JEFFERSON

STRESS IS A KILLER! In fact, the World Health Organization has named stress a world wide epidemic. So what do you do, live a stress–free life? Not in the real world, you don't. Stress is, and will continue to be, part of our business and personal lives, because situations don't always work out as we plan. So, if you can't avoid stress, what's Plan B? Manage it!

Managing stress, like many things in life, is a very personal thing. I can only share with you what works best for me, and I hope you can relate.

Number one on my list is exercise. If you've ever heard me speak or read one of my other books, you know how important exercise is to me in maintaining my attitude. It bears repeating. If I don't exercise on a regular basis, my attitude suffers and my stress levels increase. A positive attitude is tied to your energy levels. And energy (at least for me), is directly tied to exercise. The increased oxygen and endorphins in your body can be "stress busters."

What can you do to help yourself commit to exercising on a regular basis? Two suggestions: Join a health club. For me having a place to go where others are sweating just as much as I am is "comforting." I try to work out at least three mornings a week. It makes a world of difference in how I feel. Secondly, I highly recommend John Peterson's illustrated book, *Pushing Yourself to Power*. The no–equipment exercise program works great for those times when I don't have time to go to the health club or when I'm traveling.

To manage stress I also must take time for myself. No cell phones, no email, and no schedules. Just me and nature, or just me and a good book, or just me and my fishing rod or golf clubs . . . you get the idea. Quiet time helps me recharge my battery and reconnect with my soul. The key here is to plan for it, because it won't happen on its own. Even if we love our work, and I do, we need to relearn how to play and relax. I recently read an article by Al Gini titled "Don't Just Do Something, Sit There." In the article Gini noted, "Adults need play in the same way that children need play in order to fulfill themselves as people."

So, whether your personal game plan for managing stress calls for exercise, recreation, long walks, working in the garden, or reading a good book . . . just do it. It is an investment in your health, just like saving money is an investment in your financial security. Remember . . . get it, before it gets you!

LIVE IN *Awe*

Years may wrinkle the skin, but to give up enthusiasm wrinkles the soul.

SAMUEL ULLMAN

YOU CAN NEVER STEP INTO THE SAME RIVER TWICE. Like that river your past is gone and the future is promised to no one. *All you have is now.*

Jim Valvano amassed an impressive career as a basketball coach and commentator, including when his North Carolina State team beat heavily favored Houston to win the NCAA national championship in 1983. But when he was awarded the Arthur Ashe Award for Courage in 1993, it had nothing to do with basketball. Valvano had incurable cancer and had been given less than six months to live. He ended his acceptance speech with these words:

"I urge all of you to enjoy your life. Every precious moment you have on this earth. Spend each day with some laughter. Don't be afraid to feel . . . to get your emotions going. Be enthusiastic, because nothing great can be accomplished without enthusiasm. Live your dreams."

SING YOUR
SONG

A BIRD DOES NOT SING

BECAUSE IT HAS AN ANSWER.

IT SINGS BECAUSE IT HAS A SONG.

CHINESE PROVERB

Jim Valvano lived with passion and loved his life . . . he lived in awe.

A few months ago, a friend sent me a copy of an essay written by Samuel Ullman in 1920. It's called "Youth" and the words stirred my soul like nothing I've read in a long time. I'll share it with you:

Youth is not a time of life; it is a state of mind; it is not a matter of rosy cheeks, red lips and supple knees; it is a matter of the will, a quality of the imagination, a vigor of the emotions, it is the freshness of the deep springs of life.

Youth means a temperamental predominance of courage over timidity of the appetite, for adventure over the love of ease. This often exists in a man of 60 more than a boy of 20. Nobody grows old merely by a number of years. We grow old by deserting our ideals.

Years may wrinkle the skin, but to give up enthusiasm wrinkles the soul. Worry, fear, self–distrust bows the heart and turns the spirit back to dust.

Whether 60 or 16, there is in every human being's heart the lure of wonder, the unfailing childlike appetite of what's next and the joy of the game of living. In the center of your heart and my heart there is a wireless station; so long as it receives messages of beauty, hope, cheer, courage and power from men and from God, so long are you young.

When the aerials are down, and your spirit is covered with snows of cynicism and pessimism, then you are grown old, even at 20, but as long as your aerials are up, to catch waves of optimism, there is hope you may die young at 80.

Look at everything as though you are seeing it for the first time,
with eyes of a child, fresh with wonder.

JOSEPH CORNELL

PEOPLE ARE LIKE

STICKS OF DYNAMITE . . .

THE POWER'S ON THE INSIDE,

EMOTIONS

BUT NOTHING HAPPENS

UNTIL THE FUSE

GETS LIT.

USE
Emotional Triggers

WHAT IS AN "EMOTIONAL TRIGGER?" Simply put, it's a deliberate act that can stir your emotions and change the way you feel. It can be a very powerful and effective technique if you understand how and when to use it.

For example, in Chapter 7, page 38, I shared a letter with you that I wrote to myself to motivate me during a summer job in college. Each time I felt doubts, the letter would reassure me that I could succeed. It gave me instant courage and confidence to push on when I wanted to quit. Also, in Chapter 8, page 42, I shared the "one–minute laugh theory." Laughing is an emotional trigger that can sweep away negative thoughts and usher in a positive outlook.

Different triggers will work for different people. Your main trigger might be a love letter from your spouse, a card from your child, or a passage from your favorite book. Your triggers are personal, as unique as you are.

One of my most powerful triggers is music . . . words and sounds that speak to my soul and affect the way I feel. I've created a special tape that I use if I sense my attitude heading in the wrong direction. On this tape are three songs, and each has a very personal meaning. I'll get in the car, put in the tape, turn it up as loud as my eardrums can manage, and then . . . sing along. And by the way, even if you can't sing (and I definitely can't) singing along is key, because hearing and expressing the words has a "double barrel" effect on attitude. I'll share my songs with you and explain why each has a special meaning to me.

1. "What A Wonderful World," performed by Louis Armstrong. This beautiful song reminds me to live with gratitude and to be thankful for all the beauty God has placed in this world.

2. "The Wind Beneath My Wings," performed by Bette Midler. This song reminds me of my Dad—how much he did for me, and how much I loved him. He's been gone for more than twenty years, but his inspiration lives on through the beautiful words of this song. "Did you ever know that you were my hero? . . ."

3. "I Hope You Dance," performed by Lee Ann Womack. In *The Nature of Success* I explained how hearing the words to this song gave me the courage and inspiration I needed to make some difficult choices in my life. It still works.

Try it. Make your own personal tape or CD to stir your soul when stirring is needed. Here's one important key, however . . . *use it sparingly,* only when you need it, or it will lose its effect.

Music is to the soul as sunshine is to flowers.

PEACE

GOD GRANT ME THE SERENITY TO ACCEPT

THE THINGS I CANNOT CHANGE,

THE COURAGE TO CHANGE THE THINGS I CAN,

AND THE WISDOM TO KNOW THE DIFFERENCE.

REINHOLD NIEBUHR

UNLOAD YOUR *Emotional Baggage*

OUR EMOTIONS ARE POWERFUL MOTIVATORS, and more than almost anything else in our lives they will drive our behavior. Sometimes our greatest challenge is to get inside our own heads to understand what makes us tick. Why do we feel and behave the way we do?

Highly motivated, positive people are focused. The mind is clear, and energy levels are high. Also, many things can hold you back and prevent you from becoming all you can be. One of those things is . . . Emotional Baggage.

I know two family members who were best friends, but several years ago, one reminded the other of something that had happened thirty years earlier. One thing led to another and, you know what, they haven't spoken since.

Anger or resentment is like a cancer, and when you let it go untreated, it will put an invisible ceiling on your future. You don't know it . . . but it does.

William Ward identified the cure when he said, "Forgiveness is the key that unlocks the handcuffs of hate."

Those are powerful words, and I know from personal experience . . . forgiveness works. A few times in my life I've been greatly wronged and taken advantage of. My first reaction, of course, was anger and resentment. I held it for awhile and felt my stomach tie up in knots, my appetite wane, and the joy slip out of my life. The quote from Ward provided the wake–up call I needed to forgive the person who had wronged me. It was like I had been playing the first half of a basketball game with three–pound steel shoes, and in the locker room the coach said, "Mac, try these new Nikes in the second half." Multiply that by ten and you'll understand how great it feels to unload your "emotional baggage" through the power of forgiveness.

Forgiveness is the key that unlocks the handcuffs of hate.

WILLIAM WARD

FORGIVENESS

SIMPLIFY

THINGS THAT MATTER

MOST MUST NEVER BE AT

THE MERCY OF THINGS

THAT MATTER LEAST.

GOETHE

Do More
WITH LESS

ONE OF THE CONCLUSIONS I'VE REACHED as I've grown older and, I hope, wiser is that . . . *less is usually more.* In other words, when given the opportunity to simplify your life. . . take it.

I compare it to pruning a tree. By removing the excess branches the tree has more energy to bear beautiful blossoms and healthy fruit. Your life is no different. When you continually prune the areas not bearing fruit, you will be able to focus your energy on what matters most.

Granted, "simplifying your life" means many things to different people. It can mean more time, less stress, less clutter, fewer bills, and greater peace of mind. Your personal quest for simplicity may include one or all of these attributes. However, I can only share with you what has worked for me, and I hope you can relate. Consider these suggestions:

Say goodbye to "the Joneses"—Chasing symbols of success can be an all–consuming, hollow existence. Your focus on living in a larger house, driving a more luxurious car, joining the right clubs, and updating your wardrobe will bear no fruit when it comes to peace of mind. Before you make your next purchase, ask yourself these simple questions: Is this something I really need? Can I do without it? Will it make a positive difference in my life?

Live by the 80/20 Rule—In business, there's a rule of thumb that twenty percent of the sales people will generate eighty percent of the business, and that twenty percent of your customers will create eighty percent of your problems. I've found both to be true. I'm suggesting that you apply the rule to your personal life. First, identify the twenty percent of problems that create eighty percent of your stress in life. Then, focus on resolving that twenty percent. You'll be amazed at how much better you'll feel by making progress on these major issues. I also predict you'll get a boost in attitude from just making the list.

Unload your emotional baggage—As I discussed in Chapter 15, page 70, hate, anger, and resentment can lower an invisible ceiling on your future. Repeat to yourself the words of William Ward, "Forgiveness is the key that unlocks the handcuffs of hate."

Many books are available on the subject of simplifying your life, and I recommend you get one. But until you do, start your journey with these three suggestions. You and your attitude will thank me for it.

Focus on the critical few . . .
not the insignificant many.

FOCUS

THE SECRET OF GENIUS
IS TO CARRY THE SPIRIT
OF THE CHILD
INTO OLD AGE.

A CHILD'S

SPIRIT

PRACTICE
Sandbox Wisdom

IMAGINATION

*In the beginner's
mind there are
many possibilities.
In the expert's mind,
there are few.*

CHINESE PROVERB

TWO YEARS AGO my five–year–old nephew, Colin, was staying over for the weekend and we were playing his favorite game, "Giant Crab." I was the crab, giant pinchers and all. As we scuffled on the sofa, he all of a sudden looked up with loving eyes at the loose skin under my neck (those over fifty can better relate to this story) and said with childlike honesty, "Uncle Mac, you know what . . . your skin is just too big for your body." I laughed and thought to myself . . . this is classic Sandbox Wisdom.

You see, the previous weekend I had met speaker and author Tom Asacker at a convention. He came up after I spoke to give me a copy of his book *Sandbox Wisdom*. Every once in a while, a book changes the way you think, and this was one of those times. Tom, through simple truths and a beautiful story, does a remarkable job demonstrating how the importance of human connections is what life and business are all about. Providing common sense wisdom through the eyes of a child, he shows how we can revitalize our work, our relationships, and our lives. With my nephew Colin, for example, his wonderful curiosity and honesty led him to say what he did.

In addition to curiosity and honesty, let's revisit our childhood to see what we should strive to rekindle as adults.

Fun, Laughter, and Enthusiasm . . . We should strive to keep that childlike spirit in our work and our play. When we grow up we take ourselves way too seriously, and sometimes we become a heart attack waiting to happen.

No Limit Thinking . . . As children we believe that we might become president, a great artist or a great explorer. But as adults we begin to put fences around those dreams.

No Inhibitions . . . Children speak from the heart, and as adults we should strive to do more of that.

Read People and Situations . . . Children can see past the trappings of material success and see into the core of people. As we grow older we begin to label people, and as the saying goes, "labeling is disabling."

Creativity and Imagination . . . A great philosopher once observed, "Genius is childhood recaptured at will." The imagination and creativity we had at five too often begins to fade at fifteen.

If you wish to rekindle your attitude, if you desire to re–ignite passion and creativity in your life, here's some good advice . . . Practice Sandbox Wisdom.

KINDNESS

I EXPECT TO PASS THROUGH THIS
LIFE BUT ONCE. IF, THEREFORE,
THERE CAN BE ANY KINDNESS I
CAN SHOW, OR ANY GOOD THING
I CAN DO TO ANY FELLOW BEING,
LET ME DO IT NOW, FOR I SHALL
NOT RETURN THIS WAY AGAIN.

WILLIAM PENN

UNDERSTAND THE POWER OF *Humility*

SOME PEOPLE equate humility with weakness. It is just the opposite. Humility is a magnetic force that attracts goodwill from people, and it honors those who possess it.

Think of people who you met and thought, "Wow! What a wonderful human being!" I can almost guarantee you that their humility made you think that. Humility is not an act, but an attitude. It's an attitude of serving and caring for others more than you care about yourself. And those who achieve humility usually are blessed beyond their wildest dreams.

A humble person is always a great listener, and without question one of the simplest acts of kindness and humility is to listen sincerely to what someone says. I recently heard this great definition for listening: "Listening is wanting to hear." It's an emotional process, not a physical act.

Gallup took a poll of more than one million employees, and of those who thought they had a great boss, guess what was ranked as the number one reason? You got it . . . their willingness to listen to what you had to say. And I'd be willing to bet if someone took a poll among spouses, you'd get the same result!

This simple two–step formula will help you perfect the art of listening.

It is listen, ask a question:

Listen–Ask   *Listen–Ask*   *Listen–Ask*

But many people use a different two–step process:

Hear–Talk   *Hear–Talk*   *Hear–Talk*

Remember the definition . . . Listening is *wanting* to hear.

The measure of a truly great man is the
courtesy with which he treats lesser men.

ANONYMOUS

GREATNESS

FRIENDSHIP

A TRUE FRIEND IS SOMEONE

WHO CAN MAKE US DO

WHAT WE CAN.

RALPH WALDO EMERSON

Build
TRUSTED RELATIONSHIPS

WHEN FACING ADVERSITY we all need help. I've met a lot of people in my life, but I've yet to meet anyone who doesn't occasionally have fears and self–doubt. The question is not if you're going to have fear, the question is how do you react to it? One of the most critical issues in maintaining a positive attitude during adversity is to have positive people to whom you can turn. They'll give you strength and self–confidence to fight on.

Over the past thirty years, I've experienced many peaks and valleys and have usually turned to trusted friends when times got toughest.

I am a part of all that I have met.

ALFRED LORD

TENNYSON

The first is Michael McKee. Mike is the senior vice president of creative at Successories. I've known him for twenty–three years and have always depended on him to speak from his heart. I consider him a soul mate in many ways . . . someone I truly trust and respect. His ability to sort out the clutter, his insight, and his wisdom have been invaluable through the years.

Next is Peter Walts. He was with Successories for fifteen years in various management roles. When I was down Peter was a great listener and his enthusiasm was always contagious. No matter what the situation, Peter's words would give me courage and strength to fight the battles that entrepreneurs experience.

And then there's my friend Shay Coyle. I've known him for over twenty years. He owns his own accounting firm, and he is without question, one of the brightest and most down–to–earth people I've ever met. He has the ability to simplify and explain complex issues—a rare gift in the business world.

Had it not been for these friends and others like Scott Morrison, Warren Brubaker, Paul and Hans Rubens, there would be no Successories today, because I didn't have the strength and the wisdom to fight the battles alone.

Many others in business and in life have leaned on their valued relationships for strength. In 1974, Fred Smith's dream of building Federal Express was crumbling. He had exhausted his savings and the money from investors, and he owed the bank millions of dollars. Fred was ready to call it quits when he called a meeting with the bank chairman. The older gentleman, with whom Fred had developed a friendship, had been through a lot himself when he was a prisoner in a Japanese war camp. During his meeting with Fred, he kept repeating, "All things are possible to him who believes"(Mark 9:23). From that meeting, Fred found renewed strength and courage to continue to pursue his dream. Even though the business was losing millions he continued to believe . . . although most people in the business community told him it would never work. The company first turned a profit in July 1975, and in fiscal year 2003 it posted $22.5 billion in revenue.

Ken Blanchard, in his book *The Servant Leader,* says we all need "truth–tellers" in our lives. Trusted relationships provide our greatest opportunities to stay positive, to stay focused, and to grow.

ASPIRATIONS

YOUR DREAMS

AND YOUR ATTITUDE

WILL DETERMINE

YOUR ALTITUDE IN LIFE.

OUR ASPIRATIONS ARE
Our Possibilities

*To accomplish great
things we must
not only act,
but also dream;
not only plan,
but also believe.*

ANATOLE FRANCE

The Young Eagle *By Tom Reilly*

The nest of young eagles hung on every word as the Master Eagle described his exploits. This was an important day for the eaglets. They were preparing for their first solo flight from the nest. It was the confidence builder many of them needed to fulfill their destiny.

"How far can I travel?" asked one of the eaglets.

"How far can you see?" responded the Master Eagle.

"How high can I fly?" quizzed the young eaglet.

"How far can you stretch your wings?" asked the old eagle.

"How long can I fly?" the eaglet persisted.

"How far is the horizon?" the mentor rebounded.

"How much should I dream?" asked the eaglet.

"How much can you dream?" smiled the older, wiser eagle.

"How much can I achieve?" the young eagle continued.

"How much can you believe?" the old eagle challenged.

Frustrated by the banter, the young eagle demanded, "Why don't you answer my questions?"

"I did."

"Yes. But you answered them with questions."

"I answered them the best I could."

"But you're the Master Eagle. You're supposed to know everything. If you can't answer these questions, who can?"

"You." The old wise eagle reassured.

"Me? How?" the young eagle was confused.

"No one can tell you how high to fly or how much to dream. It's different for each eagle. Only God and you know how far you'll go. No one on this earth knows your potential or what's in your heart. You alone will answer that. The only thing that limits you is the edge of your imagination."

The young eagle puzzled by this asked, "What should I do?"

"Look to the horizon, spread your wings, and fly."

What could I add to these inspiring words other than say, "Thanks, Tom, for writing them."

PRIORITIES

OUR GREATEST DANGER
IN LIFE IS IN PERMITTING
THE URGENT THINGS
TO CROWD OUT
THE IMPORTANT.

CHARLES E. HUMMEL

USE OR LOSE
Your Marbles

NOTHING SHAPES OUR ATTITUDES MORE than focusing on our priorities, because when we move toward our reason for being, the result usually is happiness and peace of mind.

I recently read an article about a man who knew how to keep a good perspective on his priorities. He called it his "theory of a thousand marbles." At age 55, he began to realize his weeks and his years were flying by. He figured that the average person lived to be 75, which gave him another twenty years, so with fifty–two weeks in a year that gave him approximately one thousand precious weekends left to enjoy with the people he loved most.

So he bought one thousand marbles, put them in a clear plastic container, and placed the container on a credenza in his office. Every Monday, he would take out one marble and throw it away.

He discovered that as the marbles diminished, he focused more on the most important aspects of life, and he observed, "There's nothing like watching your time here on earth run out to help get your priorities straight."

During the past year, I've gotten to know Lance Wubbels. Lance is a terrific writer and a great person. About a year ago, he gave me a small gift book that he had just written for Hallmark, titled: *If Only I Knew*. The book is filled with gentle reminders to focus us on what matters most. Here's a sampling of what Lance had to say:

If Only I Knew . . .

This was our last hug,
I would hold you tight
And hope to never let you go.

If Only I Knew . . .

That even when everything in my life
Seems to go wrong
And comes crumbling down around me,
Even when my heart is broken,
God has promised
To always be with me.

Ah, yes . . . If we only knew, we would treasure special people in our life even more. Every day could be our last. And you might have heard it before, but it bears repeating . . . "On your deathbed, you will not say, 'I wish I had spent more time at the office.'"

The love of your family, your friends, and your faith will shape your attitude and determine your true success in life.

A man travels the world over in search of what he needs
and returns home to find it.

GEORGE MOORE

PRIORITIES

CLARITY

THE 30-Minute THEORY

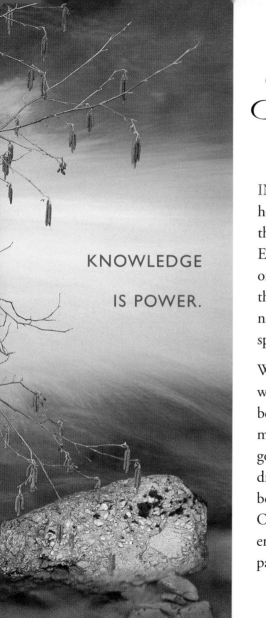

KNOWLEDGE

IS POWER.

IN MY BOOK *The Nature of Success,* I shared how my friend Jim Cathcart became one of the top speakers in the country by applying Earl Nightingale's philosophy of spending one hour a day pursuing your goal. If you did this, Nightingale said, you could become a national expert in five years. Jim, with no speaking experience, proved him right.

Well, sometimes we have to crawl before we walk; therefore, I've decided to give you the benefit of the doubt to spend only thirty minutes. The challenge is simple. Identify a goal that is important to you. It could be a dream of starting your own business. It could be improving your skills in your existing job. Or it could be more personal, such as enhancing your spiritual life, being a better parent, or being a better spouse.

In the simplest terms, use the thirty minutes a day to seek knowledge and clarity on the goal you've selected. Secondly, understand that knowledge and clarity are power, and will help to bring this goal to life. Once you can visualize clearly, your attitude and your confidence soar. Therefore, your chances to succeed soar, too.

As you've read this, I'm sure some of you have already wondered, "Where do I get thirty minutes? My life is going a hundred miles an hour." Those who immediately dismissed the thirty–minute theory might need some advice from a Greek philosopher:

A young man approached the sage and said, "I've come to you for knowledge." The philospher nodded, took the young man by the hand, and led him to a river nearby. Together they waded into the currents, and the teacher looked at the young man and said, "Hold my arm." He then dunked the inquirer's head under the water for about twenty seconds. When the young man came up, the teacher asked again, "What have you come here for?" The young man repeated, "I've come to you for knowledge." The philosopher dunked him again and this time held him down much longer. As he came up, the sage asked yet again, "What do you want?" The young man sputtered, "Give me air! Give me air!" The philosopher then said, "When you want knowledge as much as you want air, you shall have it."

Now that the sage has shared some of his less–than–subtle insight, you might wish to rethink your problem with finding thirty minutes for self–improvement. If you want it badly enough you can either: (a) set the alarm thirty minutes earlier or (b) sacrifice thirty minutes of television time each night. As the saying goes, "You'll never get what you've never had until you're willing to do what you've never done." Discipline and commitment are key to accomplishing anything worthwhile in your life.

For example, if your goal is to start your own business, here's some practical advice—become an amateur before you turn pro. Use your thirty minutes a day to read all you can that will prepare you for the journey. Think about it: Thirty minutes a day is over one hundred eighty hours a year. Can you imagine how much knowledge you could gain in all that time? Assume the average book takes you four hours to read; that's about forty–five books a year. I recommend you start with the biographies of great entrepreneurs of our time—people like Sam Walton (Wal–Mart), Steve Jobs (Apple), Fred Smith (Federal Express), Ray Kroc (McDonald's), Howard Shultz (Starbucks), and others. Their insights about the choices they made, their values, their commitment to hiring the best people, their passion for serving customers, and their battles to overcome adversity would help you build a foundation for entrepreneurial success.

Remember, knowledge is power. It gives you the self–confidence to make difficult choices in life and to stay positive in times of adversity.

LOVE

I WISH YOU *Love*

> LOVE DOESN'T MAKE
>
> THE WORLD GO ROUND.
>
> LOVE IS WHAT MAKES
>
> THE RIDE WORTHWHILE.
>
> FRANKLIN P. JONES

AUGUST 1992. Derrick Redmond from Great Britain was favored to win the 400–meter race during the summer Olympic Games in Barcelona, Spain. But as he powered around the backstretch his hamstring snapped. Derrick tried desperately to finish the race, but he still had half the distance to go. Because he couldn't walk, he began to hop. One step—a grimace. Two steps—a yell.

Jim Redmond had to get to his struggling son. He doesn't remember all the steps down from Section 131, Row 22, Seat 25 of the Olympic Stadium. He doesn't really remember leaping over the railing or pushing off security guards who were too stunned to stop him. He was not just a spectator at the Olympics anymore; Jim Redmond was a father, and he had to get to his son.

"Dad," Derrick said, "Dad . . . Get me back to lane five. I want to finish."

And leaning on each other, father and son made their way around the track as the crowd, with the whole world watching, rose to their feet cheering. Olympic organizers can light the skies with fireworks, they can invite kings and queens . . . but this was the magic of real life.

That day people saw an example of great courage, but they witnessed an even greater story about love.

Love, simply stated, is the essence of life. It can put the smile on your face, the bounce in your step, and most importantly, the joy in your heart. Even when your whole world is crumbling around you, one person holding your hand, looking into your eyes, saying "I love you" is enough to get you through.

Love is to attitude as the rain is to flowers. Surround yourself with people who love you, and whom you can love back. This, more than anything else you can do, will provide the music for your life and the fuel for your soul.

Just recently a friend included a wonderful poem by Robert Ward in her letter to me. I hope you like it as much as I did.

I wish you the courage to be warm when the world
     Would prefer that you be cool.
     I wish you success sufficient to your needs;
     I wish you failure to temper that success.
I wish you joy in all your days; I wish you sadness
     So that you may better measure that joy.
I wish you gladness to overbalance grief.
I wish you humor and a twinkle in the eye.
I wish you glory and the strength to bear its burdens.
I wish you sunshine on your path and storms to season
     Your journey.
I wish you peace in the world in which you live and in the
     Smallest corner of the heart where truth is kept.
I wish you faith to help define your living and your life.
More I cannot wish you, except perhaps love, to make
     All the rest worthwhile.

ATTITUDE

YOU BECOME WHAT
YOU THINK ABOUT.

EARL NIGHTINGALE

THE *Choice* IS YOURS

LATE ONE AFTERNOON a skinny young man dashed down the steps at his school to check out the bulletin board by the gym. His heart was pounding as he saw the list that would tell if he had realized his dream of making the high school basketball team. He read it again and again, each time with the same result—his name was not there. He had failed. That day, that moment, would change his life.

For the next year, regardless of the weather, he practiced four to six hours every day in a park about a mile from his home. Many nights he was alone under the moonlight, practicing every move, every shot that he needed to make next year's team.

The ending is a happy one. He did make the team—and Michael Jordan, on the heels of failure, went on to become the greatest basketball player of all time.

What is the lesson to be learned from the Michael Jordan story? It is this . . . your success or failure in life will not be decided by the number of setbacks you encounter, but rather how you react to them. Jordan had a choice. He could take his defeat personally, blame the coach, and throw in the towel, or he could do what he did—keep working, keep trying. Would Jordan ever have achieved greatness had he not fought back from failure? My guess is no. I believe with all my heart that, "Whatever doesn't kill us makes us stronger." If you choose a positive approach in difficult times, you can take control of your life.

Of all the material I've ever read about the importance of maintaining a positive attitude, this classic essay from Charles Swindoll is my favorite.

The longer I live, the more I realize the impact of attitude on life. Attitude, to me, is more important than the facts.

It is more important than the past, than education, than money, than circumstances, than failures, than successes, than what other people think or say or do. It is more important than appearance, giftedness, or skill. It will make or break a company . . . a church . . . a home.

The remarkable thing is we have a choice every day regarding the attitude we will embrace for that day. We cannot change our pasts, we cannot change the fact that people will act in a certain way. We cannot change the inevitable. The only thing we can do is play on the one string we have, and that is our attitude.

I am convinced that life is 10 percent what happens to me and 90 percent how I react to it. And so it is with you—we are in charge of our attitudes.

*Your success or failure in life will not be decided
by the number of setbacks you encounter,
but rather how you react to them.*

KNOWLEDGE

THE KEY TO SUCCESS IN LIFE

IS USING THE GOOD

THOUGHTS OF WISE PEOPLE.

LEO TOLSTOY

FIND A *Mentor*

NOTHING BOOSTS your self-confidence or nurtures your positive attitude more than a mentor. And remember this . . . you're never too old or too young to have one.

The ability to find and benefit from a mentor is one of the key lessons to be drawn from the extraordinary life of Eleanor Roosevelt. As Robin Gerber, author of *Leadership the Eleanor Roosevelt Way*, explains: Great mentors "will not only lead you on your future professional path but also help you to realize your full potential—spiritually, mentally, emotionally."

Eleanor did not have a happy childhood. After losing her parents at a young age, she had no one to show her any respect or affection. And because she was unattractive and lacked certain social graces, her own family members—not to mention other children—insulted and ridiculed her.

Ordinarily such a childhood would lead to a lack of self–esteem and confidence. Nothing, as we all know, was further from the truth. She was not afraid to fly in the face of convention, to do exactly as she pleased with the whole world watching. How did the shy, unattractive girl become the smiling, confident Eleanor Roosevelt?

Much of the success of this great lady has to do with another lady—a mentor she met in boarding school. Marie Souvestre was the French headmistress of the English boarding school to which Roosevelt was sent when she was 15 years old. Instead of laughing at Roosevelt, Souvestre encouraged and complimented Eleanor on her intellect, her proficiency in the French language, and her attitude toward the other girls. Slowly, Souvestre built up young Eleanor's confidence, in essence creating the young woman who later would take on the world.

Ask yourself who could make a positive difference in your life. When faced with difficult choices or challenges, to whom could you turn for guidance? The answer might not come to you immediately, and that's probably for the best. What I would suggest is that you go through your address books and make a list of candidates. List the strengths and weaknesses of each person, and rank potential mentors in the order of preference. At that point, I'd arrange a lunch with your top choice (or send a letter) to gauge their interest. You might be surprised at how flattered some people are that you asked; however, if a mentoring relationship doesn't work out, move to your second choice. I've always lived by the "nothing ventured, nothing gained" theory, and selecting a mentor is one place to put it to the test.

I also suggest you read books specifically about mentoring relationships, but for now I hope I've helped you take that first step. The right mentor can change your life in many positive ways.

PURPOSE

YOUR VISION

BECOMES CLEAR

WHEN YOU LOOK

INSIDE YOUR HEART.

WHO LOOKS

OUTSIDE, DREAMS.

WHO LOOKS

INSIDE, AWAKENS.

CARL JUNG

Know THYSELF

"YOU HAVE TO *BE*, before you *do*, to have lasting inner peace." In other words, making a living is not the same as making a life. Find what makes your heart sing and create your own music.

Many people work all their lives and dislike what they do for a living. In fact, I was astounded to see a recent *USA Today* survey that said fifty-three percent of people in the American workplace are unhappy with their jobs. Loving what you do is one of the most important keys to maintaining a positive attitude. You can't fake passion. It is the fuel that drives any dream and makes you happy to be alive. However, to love what you do, the first step is to self–analyze, to simply know what you love. We all have unique talents and interests, and one of life's greatest

Throw your heart over the fence and the rest will follow.

NORMAN VINCENT PEALE

challenges is to match these talents with career opportunities that bring out the best in us. It's not easy—and sometimes we can only find it through trial and error—but it's worth the effort.

Ray Kroc, for example, found his passion when he founded McDonald's at the age of 52. He never "worked" another day of his life.

John James Audubon was unsuccessful for most of his life. He was a terrible businessman. No matter how many times he changed locations, changed partners, or changed businesses, he still failed miserably.

Not until he understood that he must change himself did he have any shot at success.

And what changes did Audubon make? He followed his passion. He always had loved the outdoors and was an excellent hunter. In addition, he was a good artist and as a hobby would draw local birds.

Once he stopped trying to be a businessman and started doing what he loved to do, his life turned around. He traveled the country observing and drawing birds, and

his art ultimately was collected in a book titled *Audubon's Birds of America*. The book earned him a place in history as the greatest wildlife artist ever. But more importantly, the work made him happy and provided the peace of mind he'd been seeking all his life.

How do you find your purpose in life? There are no easy answers, but here are two practical tips that can help:

1. *Discover Your Gifts*—We're all unique and each of us has our own special gifts. Make a list of what you consider your strengths and your weaknesses. Next, don't just assume your assumptions are correct. Get feedback from what Ken Blanchard calls "trusted truth–tellers"—friends and family members who won't just tell you what you want to hear but who will share their true opinions. With their help you can get a realistic perspective of your gifts.

2. *Discover What Moves You*—Find your passion and strive to live your life around it. Make your list. Do your homework. There is this caution, however . . . have patience. Your purpose in life probably won't surface overnight, but like love, it will find you when you least expect it.

Finding your reason for being brings a positive attitude that can be unstoppable.

RENEWAL

THE WILL TO WIN . . . THE WILL TO ACHIEVE . . . GOES
DRY AND ARID WITHOUT CONTINUOUS RENEWAL.

VINCE LOMBARDI, JR.

Reinforce,
REINFORCE, REINFORCE

I'M SURE YOU'VE HEARD THE THREE KEYS to purchasing real estate . . . location, location, location. Well, you'll now hear the three keys to managing your attitude . . . reinforce, reinforce, reinforce. Zig Ziglar remarked, "People often say to me that motivation doesn't last. Well, neither does bathing . . . that's why we recommend it daily."

What a great quote! I'm often amazed that some people think that because I am who I am, I must have a great attitude at all times. "You started Successories. You couldn't possibly have a negative thought!" Well, here's a confession. One of the main reasons I started Successories is that I saw the need for continuous reinforcement in my life and in others when it comes to attitude, goals, and values.

In a perfect world, we hear something once, record it in our brain, and never need to hear it again. Well, I don't know where you're living, but my world is far from perfect. I occasionally have doubts, fears, and disappointments in my life. During those times I need "shots of inspiration" to reinforce, to encourage, and to motivate.

What are some ways to reinforce what you believe, or to help you stay positive? Again, it's a very personal thing, but for me good books, "feel good" movies, music, prayer, exercise, and spending quality time with a positive friend can all make a difference. One of the keys, however, is not to wait until you get "down" to act. You need to make the time to *reinforce* on a daily, weekly, and monthly basis. Understanding the need is a first step. A proactive plan, however, is necessary to make reinforcement happen.

In his book *What It Takes To Be #1,* Vince Lombardi, Jr. said, "'Continuous renewal' is an umbrella term for anything you can do to keep in touch with your values and your life purpose. This is a discipline that all successful people fashion for themselves. The will to win—the will to achieve—goes dry and arid without continuous renewal."

I'LL END AS I BEGAN . . . attitude is a little thing that makes a big difference. It is my hope that you'll use this book as a tool to provide that "shot of inspiration" and continuous reinforcement you'll need to stay positive. And never forget . . . attitudes truly are contagious, so decide today to make yours worth catching.

Attitudes are nothing more than habits of thoughts,
and habits can be acquired.
An action repeated becomes an attitude realized.

PAUL MYER

MENTAL HABITS

"My personal thanks to Bruce Heinemann and Steve Terrill. Their breathtaking photography is second to none ... but more importantly, they are great people who live with passion." (Mac)

BRUCE W. HEINEMANN has photographed the American landscape for over twenty–five years. He is the photographer of the critically acclaimed book *The Art of Nature: Reflections on the Grand Design.* He also authored and photographed *A Guide To Photographing The Art of Nature.* Both were Book of the Month Club feature selections and best-sellers. His most recent publication, *The Four Seasons* book and music CD, has met with great acclaim. Bruce's photos appear on pages 4, 16, 24, 44, 61, 72, 88, 100, 108, 126 of *The Power of Attitude.*

For more information, please visit www.theartofnature.com.

STEVE TERRILL, a native of Portland, Oregon, has been trekking throughout the United States since 1980 with his main focus on the Great Northwest. Since then, his work has been published in numerous magazines, calendars, and books, including more than twenty of his own titles. He was the featured photographer in the gift books *The Wonder of It All* and *How Majestic is Thy Name,* which won the Christian Booksellers Association's Gold Medallion award in 2001 and 2002 respectively. Steve's photos appear on pages 2, 32, 36, 68, 76, 112, 116, 120 of *The Power of Attitude.*

For more information, please visit www.terrillphoto.com.

MAC ANDERSON is the founder of Simple Truths and Successories, Inc., the leader in designing and marketing products for motivation and recognition. These companies, however, are not the first success stories for Mac. He was also the founder and CEO of McCord Travel, the largest travel company in the Midwest, and part owner/VP of sales and marketing for Orval Kent Food Company, the country's largest manufacturer of prepared salads.

His accomplishments in these unrelated industries provide some insight into his passion and leadership skills. He also brings the same passion to his speaking where he speaks to many corporate audiences on avariety of topics, including leadership, motivation, and team building.

Mac has authored or co-authored thirteen books that have sold over three million copies. His titles include: *Charging the Human Battery, Customer Love, Motivational Quotes, Finding Joy, You Can't Send a Duck to Eagle School, 212°: The Extra Degree, Learning to Dance in the Rain, Change is Good … You Go First, The Nature of Success, The Power of Attitude, The Essence of Leadership, To a Child, Love is Spelled T-I-M-E, The Dash and What's the Big Idea?*

For more information, please visit www.simpletruths.com

Gift Books by Mac Anderson

THE POWER OF ATTITUDE
Hardcover, 128 pages, 6.75" square, $15.95

This combines award winning photography, inspirational quotes, and real life stories that will help you manage your attitude in business and life. A Gift That Will ENERGIZE Outlooks and Transform Attitudes.

THE NATURE OF SUCCESS
Hardcover, 128 pages, 6.75" square, $15.95

This award winning gift book shares Mac's 28 principles of success in an unforgettable way. Learn to define goals, manage attitude, embrace change and make a difference whenever and wherever possible.

212°, THE EXTRA DEGREE
By Sam Parker and Mac Anderson
Hardcover, 96 pages, 6.75" square, $15.95

At 211°, water is hot. At 212°, it boils and creates steam. And steam can power a locomotive. This one extra degree makes all the difference. This book is filled with stories, quotations, and photos reinforcing the concept that one extra degree of effort in business or in life can separate the good from the great.

CUSTOMER LOVE
Hardcover, 128 pages, 6.75" square, $15.95

A must read for any business wanting to create a service culture. 24 unforgettable true stories about individuals and companies who have "wowed" their customers and turned them into raving fans.

YOU CAN'T SEND A DUCK TO EAGLE SCHOOL

Hardcover, 128 pages, 6.75" square, $15.95

A must have guide for every leader – this book will help you hire better people, become a better leader, get more done is less time and ignite your team to perform to their highest potential.

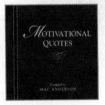

MOTIVATIONAL QUOTES

Hardcover, 160 pages, 6.75" square, $15.95

If you love quotes, you will love this book filled with 160 of Mac Anderson's favorite quotes. Keep this book close by to find the right words of encouragement at the right time.

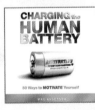

CHARGING THE HUMAN BATTERY

Hardcover, 144 pages, 6.75" square, $15.95

Recommended reading for anyone who ever feels the need to re-charge their personal or business life. Each of us has different triggers for self-motivation. Within these 50 ideas to motivate yourself, you will find many "A-ha" moments.

LEARNING TO DANCE IN THE RAIN

By BJ Gallagher and Mac Anderson
Hardcover, 112 pages, 6.75" square, $15.95

No matter what your circumstances are, you cannot read this book and not feel extremely blessed! An inspiring and beautiful gift book full of wonderful stories, quotes, poems and insight to help you reflect on the positives in life.

For more information, please visit www.simpletruths.com

The Simple Truth Difference

If you have enjoyed this book we invite you to check out our entire collection of gift books, with free inspirational movies, at **www.simpletruths.com**.

You'll discover it's a great way to inspire *friends* and *family,* or to thank your best *customers* and *employees.*

For more information, please visit us at:
www.simpletruths.com

Or call us toll free...
800-900-3427

simple truths®
THE GIFT OF INSPIRATION